The Wife

[Cover photograph by Mrs. Sharon White: "View of the back grounds at the historic Lincoln mansion in Manchester, Vermont."]

The Wife

The Legacy of Home Press Classic Edition

by Washington Irving

The text from the current edition was carefully transcribed and lightly edited from the 1881 edition of *The Sketch Book* by Washington Irving. It was originally published by:
American Book Exchange, New York.

Any additional images or text that has been added includes their source.

ISBN Number: 978-1-956616-16-3

The Legacy of Home Press

Vermont - U.S.A.

Foreword

THE following is a short story written by Washington Irving in the 1800's. It describes how one couple had a happy marriage regardless of the loss of the husband's wealth and business.

The description of how his wife continues to make a happy home even in her new found poverty is inspiring.

The Wife was originally published in a compilation of other short stories. However, we feel the story would be much appreciated in a publication of its own. The timeless message will be an inspiration to others regardless of their financial circumstances.

To this edition, we have added peaceful scenic paintings which were originally published in the 1800's. We hope these illustrations will add to the enjoyment of the story.

Mrs. Sharon White
- The Legacy of Home Press -
Vermont, 2023.

Pieter Hendrik Koekkoek painting: "A View of the Park" (1800's).

Contents

Illustrations

George Henry Durrie painting; "Winter Farmyard" (1800's).

The Wife

I HAVE often had occasion to remark the fortitude with which women sustain the most overwhelming reverses of fortune. Those disasters which break down the spirit of a man, and prostrate him in the dust, seem to call forth all the energies of the softer sex, and give such intrepidity and elevation to their character, that at times it approaches to sublimity. Nothing can be more touching, than to behold a soft and tender female, who had been all weakness and dependence, and alive to every trivial roughness, while threading the prosperous paths of life, suddenly rising in mental force to be the comforter and supporter of her husband under misfortune, and abiding with unshrinking firmness, the bitterest blasts of adversity.

George Henry Durrie painting "The Old Grist Mill" (1800's).

As the vine, which has long twined its graceful foliage about the oak, and been lifted by it into sunshine, will, when the hardy plant is rifted by the thunderbolt, cling round it with its caressing tendrils, and bind up its shattered boughs; so is it beautifully ordered by Providence, that woman, who is the mere dependent and ornament of man in his happier hours, should be his stay and solace when smitten with sudden calamity; winding herself into the rugged recesses of his nature, tenderly supporting the drooping head, and binding up the broken heart.

I was once congratulating a friend, who had around him a blooming family, knit together in the strongest affection. "I can wish you no better lot," said he, with enthusiasm, "than to have a wife and children. If you are prosperous, there they are to share your prosperity; if otherwise, there they are to comfort you." And, indeed, I have observed that a married man, falling into misfortune, is more apt to retrieve his situation in the world than a single one; partly because he is more stimulated to exertion by the necessities of the helpless and beloved beings who depend upon him for subsistence; but chiefly because his spirits are soothed and relieved by domestic endearments, and his self-respect kept alive by finding, that though all abroad is darkness and humiliation, yet there is still a little world of love at home, of which he is the monarch. Whereas, a single man is apt to run to

Pieter Hendrik Koekkoek painting "Summer Landscape" (1800's).

waste and self-neglect; to fancy himself lonely and abandoned, and his heart to fall to ruin, like some deserted mansion, for want of an inhabitant.

These observations call to mind a little domestic story, of which I was once a witness. My intimate friend, George, had married a beautiful and accomplished girl, who had been brought up in the midst of fashionable life. She had, it is true, no fortune, but that of my friend was ample; and he delighted in the anticipation of indulging her in every elegant pursuit, and administering to those delicate tastes and fancies that spread a kind of fascination about the female sex. – "Her life," said he, "shall be like a fairy tale."

The very difference in their characters produced a harmonious combination; he was of a romantic and somewhat serious cast; she was all life and gladness. I have often noticed the mute rapture with which he would gaze upon her in company, of which her sprightly powers made her the delight; and how, in the midst of applause, her eye would still turn to him, as if there alone she sought favor and acceptance. When leaning on his arm, her slender form contrasted finely with his tall, manly person. The fond confiding air with which she looked up to him seemed

George Henry Durrie painting "Haying at Jones Inn" (1800's).

to call forth a flush of triumphant pride and cherishing tenderness, as if he doted on his lovely burden for its very helplessness. Never did a couple set forward on the flowery path of early and well-suited marriage with a fairer prospect of felicity.

It was the misfortune of my friend, however, to have embarked his property in large speculations; and he had not been married many months, when, by a succession of sudden disasters, it was swept from him and he found himself reduced almost to penury. For a time he kept his situation to himself, and went about with a haggard countenance, and a breaking heart. His life was but a protracted agony; and what rendered it more insupportable was the necessity of keeping up a smile in the presence of his wife; for he could not bring himself to overwhelm her with the news. She saw, however, with the quick eyes of affection, that all was not well with him. She marked his altered looks and stifled sighs, and was not to be deceived by his sickly and vapid attempts at cheerfulness. She tasked all her sprightly powers and tender blandishments to win him back to happiness; but she only drove the arrow deeper into his soul. The more he saw cause to love her, the more torturing was the thought that he was soon to make her wretched. A little while, thought he, and the smile will vanish

George Henry Durrie painting "Winter Scene" (1800's).

from that cheek – the song will die away from those lips – the luster of those eyes will be quenched with sorrow; and the happy heart, which now beats lightly, will be weighed down like mine, by the cares and the miseries of the world.

At length, he came to me one day, and related his whole situation in a tone of the deepest despair. When I heard him through I inquired, "Does your wife know all this?" – At the question he burst into an agony of tears. "If you have any pity on me," cried he, "don't mention my wife; it is the thought of her that drives me almost to madness!"

"And why not?" said I. "She must know it sooner or later: you cannot keep it long from her, and the intelligence may break upon her in a more startling manner, than if imparted by yourself; for the accents of those we love soften the harshest tidings. Besides, you are depriving yourself of the comforts of her sympathy; and not merely that, but also endangering the only bond that can keep hearts together – an unreserved community of thought and feeling. She will soon perceive that something is secretly preying upon your mind; and true love will not brook reserve; it feels undervalued and outraged, when even the sorrows of those it loves are concealed from it."

Pieter Hendrik Koekkoek painting "A Wooded Landscape" (1800's).

"Oh, but, my friend! To think what a blow I am to give to all her future prospects – how I am to strike her very soul to the earth, by telling her that her husband is a beggar! That she is to forego all the elegancies of life – all the pleasures of society – to shrink with me into indigence and obscurity! To tell her that I have dragged her down from the sphere in which she might have contrived to move in constant brightness – the light of every eye – the admiration of every heart! – How can she bear poverty? She has been brought up in all the refinements of opulence. How can she bear neglect? She has been highly esteemed by society. Oh! It will break her heart – it will break her heart! –"

I saw his grief was eloquent, and I let it have its flow; for sorrow relieves itself by words. When his paroxysm had subsided, and he had relapsed into moody silence, I resumed the subject gently, and urged him to break his situation at once to his wife. He shook his head mournfully, but positively.

"But how are you to keep it from her? It is necessary she should know it, that you may take the steps proper to the alteration of your circumstances. You must change your style of living – nay," observing a pang to pass across his countenance, "don't let that afflict you. I am sure you have never placed your

Pieter Hendrik Koekkoek painting "Thatched Barn" (1800's).

happiness in outward show – you have yet friends, warm friends, who will not think the worse of you for being less splendidly lodged: and surely it does not require a palace to be happy with Mary –"

"I could be happy with her," cried he, convulsively, "in a hovel! – I could go down with her into poverty and the dust! – I could – I could – God bless her! – God bless her!" cried he, bursting into a transport of grief and tenderness.

"And believe me, my friend," said I, stepping up, and grasping him warmly by the hand, "believe me she can be the same with you. Aye, more: it will be a source of pride and triumph to her – it will call forth all the latent energies and fervent sympathies of her nature; for she will rejoice to prove that she loves you for yourself. There is in every true woman's heart a spark of heavenly fire, which lies dormant in the broad daylight of prosperity; but which kindles up, and beams and blazes in the dark hour of adversity. No man knows what the wife of his heart is – no man knows what a ministering angel she is – until he has gone with her through the fiery trials of this world."

Pieter Hendrik Koekkoek painting "At the Farm" (1800's).

There was something in the earnestness of my manner, and the figurative style of my language, that caught the excited imagination of George. I knew the auditor I had to deal with; and following up the impression I made, I finished by persuading him to go home and unburden his sad heart to his wife.

I must confess, notwithstanding all I had said, I felt some little solicitude for the result. Who can calculate on the fortitude of one whose life has been a round of pleasures? Her merry spirits might revolt at the dark downward path of low humility suddenly pointed out before her, and might cling to the sunny regions in which they had hitherto reveled. Besides, ruin in fashionable life is accompanied by so many galling mortifications, to which in other ranks it is a stranger. – In sort, I could not meet George the next morning without trepidation. He had made the disclosure.

"And how did she bear it?"

"Like an angel! It seemed rather to be a relief to her mind, for she threw her arms round my neck, and asked if this was all that had lately made me unhappy. – But, poor girl," added he, "she cannot realize the change we must undergo. She has no idea of

George Henry Durrie painting "Winter in the Country" (1800's).

poverty but in the abstract; she has only read of it in poetry, where it is allied to love. She feels as yet no privation; she suffers no loss of accustomed conveniences nor elegancies. When we come practically to experience its sordid cares, its paltry wants, its petty humiliations – then will be the real trial."

"But," said I, "now that you have got over the severest task, that of breaking it to her, the sooner you let the world into the secret the better. The disclosure may be mortifying; but then it is a single misery, and soon over: whereas you otherwise suffer it, in anticipation, every hour in the day. It is not poverty so much as pretence, that harasses a ruined man – the struggle between a proud mind and an empty purse – the keeping up a hollow show that must soon come to an end. Have the courage to appear poor and you disarm poverty of its sharpest sting." On this point I found George perfectly prepared. He had no false pride in himself, and as to his wife, she was only anxious to conform to their altered fortunes.

Some days afterwards he called upon me in the evening. He had disposed of his dwelling house, and taken a small cottage in the country, a few miles from town. He had been busied all day in sending out furniture. The new establishment required few

George Heny Durrie painting "View of Westville" (1800's).

articles, and those of the simplest kind. All the splendid furniture of his late residence had been sold, excepting his wife's harp. That, he said, was too closely associated with the idea of herself; it belonged to the little story of their loves; for some of the sweetest moments of their courtship were those when he had leaned over that instrument, and listened to the melting tones of her voice. I could not but smile at this instance of romantic gallantry in a doting husband.

He was now going out to the cottage, where his wife had been all day superintending its arrangement. My feelings had become strongly interested in the progress of this family story, and, as it was a fine evening, I offered to accompany him.

He was wearied with the fatigues of the day, and, as he walked out, fell into a fit of gloomy musing.

"Poor Mary!" at length broke, with a heavy sigh, from his lips.

"And what of her?" asked I: "has anything happened to her?"

Pieter Hendrik Koekkoek painting "Forest Stream" (1800's).

"What," said he, darting an impatient glance, "is it nothing to be reduced to this paltry situation – to be caged in a miserable cottage – to be obliged to toil almost in the menial concerns of her wretched habitation?"

"Has she then repined at the change?"

"Repined! She has been nothing but sweetness and good humor. Indeed, she seems in better spirits than I have ever known her; she has been to me all love, and tenderness, and comfort!"

"Admirable girl!" exclaimed I. "You call yourself poor, my friend; you never were so rich – you never knew the boundless treasures of excellence you possess in that woman."

"Oh! But, my friend, if this first meeting at the cottage were over, I think I could then be comfortable. But this is her first day of real experience; she has been introduced into a humble dwelling – she has been employed all day in arranging its miserable equipments – she has, for the first time, known the fatigues of domestic employment – she has, for the first time,

George Henry Durrie painting "Going to Church" (1800's).

looked round her on a home destitute of everything elegant, – almost of everything convenient; and may now be sitting down, exhausted and spiritless, brooding over a prospect of future poverty."

There was a degree of probability in this picture that I could not gainsay, so we walked on in silence.

After turning from the main road up a narrow lane, so thickly shaded with forest trees as to give it a complete air of seclusion, we came in sight of the cottage. It was humble enough in its appearance for the most pastoral poet; and yet it had a pleasing rural look. A wild vine had overrun one end with a profusion of foliage; a few trees threw their branches gracefully over it; and I observed several pots of flowers tastefully disposed about the door, and on the grass-plot in front. A small wicket gate opened upon a footpath that wound through some shrubbery to the door. Just as we approached, we heard the sound of music – George grasped my arm; we paused and listened. It was Mary's voice singing, in a style of the most touching simplicity, a little air of which her husband was peculiarly fond.

Daniel Ridgway Knight painting "Picking Flowers" (1800's).

I felt George's hand tremble on my arm. He stepped forward to hear more distinctly. His step made a noise on the gravel walk. A bright beautiful face glanced out at the window and vanished – a light footstep was heard and Mary came tripping forth to meet us: she was in a pretty rural dress of white; a few wild flowers were twisted in her fine hair; a fresh bloom was on her cheek; her whole countenance beamed with smiles – I had never seen her look so lovely.

"My dear George," cried she, "I am so glad you are come! I have been watching and watching for you; and running down the lane, and looking out for you. I've set out a table under a beautiful tree behind the cottage; and I've been gathering some of the most delicious strawberries, for I know you are fond of them – and we have such excellent cream – and everything is so sweet and still here – Oh!" said she, putting her arm within his, and looking up brightly in his face, "Oh, we shall be so happy!"

Poor George was overcome. He caught her close to him – he folded his arms round her – he kissed her again and again – he could not speak, but the tears gushed into his eyes; and he has

Daniel Ridgway Knight painting "Girl by a Stream" (1800's).

often assured me, that though the world has since gone prosperously with him, and his life has, indeed, been a happy one, yet never has he experienced a moment of more exquisite felicity.

~THE END ~

Daniel Ridgway Knight painting "Coffee in the Garden" (1800's).

"Not that I speak in respect of want: for I have learned, in whatsoever state I am, therewith to be content."

~ Philippians 4:11

Inspiring Christian Fiction from the 1800's:

The Legacy of Home Press classic editions by Mrs. Elizabeth Prentiss:

"Aunt Jane's Hero"

ISBN: 978-1-956616-02-6

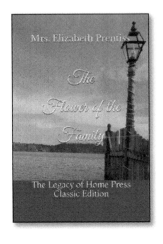

"The Flower of the Family"

ISBN: 978-1-956616-08-8

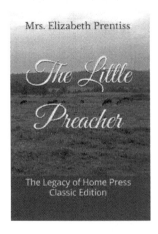

"The Little Preacher"

ISBN: 978-1-956616-10-1

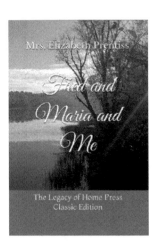

"Fred and Maria and Me"

ISBN: 978-1-956616-12-5

The Prentiss Study

90- Day Devotional Study
For a Peaceful, Old Fashioned Bible Time.

(Using the book, "Stepping Heavenward" by Mrs. Elizabeth Prentiss.)

This deluxe edition includes these special features:

~ A brief biography of the Prentiss family at their summer home in Dorset, Vermont (in the 1800's). This includes details of their family life, and photographs taken in 2019 by the author of this study, Mrs. White, when she visited Dorset a few years ago. You will see a little of the town and the Prentiss home.

~Reference notes include details of sources and other helpful information and guidance.

~The study itself has 90 days of assignments with a place to check off each item as completed. There are detailed directions with inspiring quotes from the letters of Mrs. Elizabeth Prentiss.

~This Bible study is designed for both individual and group use.

Available in both paperback and hardcover editions:

  "Prentiss Study Deluxe Edition" by Mrs. Sharon White

ISBN: 978-1956616-0-40 (paperback, 105 pages)

ISBN: 978-1956616-0-57 (hardcover, 105 pages)

Also Available:

The Legacy of Home Press classic edition by Mrs. Elizabeth Prentiss:

"Stepping Heavenward" ISBN: 978-1-956616-00-2

For more titles by The Legacy of Home Press, please visit us at:

https://thelegacyofhomepress.blogspot.com

"*Blessed is the people that know the joyful sound: they shall walk, O Lord, in the light of thy countenance.*"

~ *Psalm 89:15*

Made in the USA
Coppell, TX
23 May 2023

17186307R00024